MW00570601

The WEIGHT of a BOX

To Eden
Thank you
for your support

poems by
Laura Williams French

The Weight of a Box $10.00

Poems by Laura Williams French
Clare Songbirds Publishing House Poetry Series
ISBN 978-1-947653-34-4
Clare Songbirds Publishing House
The Weight of a Box © 2018 Laura Williams French

Printed in the United States of America
FIRST EDITION

Clare Songbirds Publishing House Mission Statement:
Clare Songbirds Publishing House was established to provide a print forum for the creation of limited edition, fine art from poets and writers, both established and emerging. We strive to reignite and continue a tradition of quality, accessible literary arts to the national and international community of writers, and readers. Chapbook manuscripts are carefully chosen for their ability to propel the expansion of art and ideas in literary form. We provide an accessible way to promote the art of words in order to resonate with, and impact, readers not yet familiar with the siren song of poets and writers. Clare Songbirds Publishing House espouses a singular cultural development where poetry creates community and becomes commonplace in public places.

140 Cottage Street
Auburn, New York 13021
www.ClareSongbirdspub.com

cover photo courtesy of Amazing Urns

Contents

For Rhonda
and Alex

"To weep is to make less the depth of grief."
~William Shakespeare

"How Old Are You?"

Asked the little girl
with big, blue eyes
and corkscrew curls

"Old enough"
I laugh
and think

How old am I?

the date on my drivers license?
and silver streaks
in my once ebon hair

as old as
arthritis
creaking in my bones

or am I

as old as
jumping in puddles
with red rubber boots

as old as
cotton candy sticky fingers
at the petting zoo

or am I

as old as
mist on the mountains
ethereal and eternal

Struck Blind

If I were struck blind
what color would you be?
without my eyes
my heart sees

voices color
a dark world
sound,
my new sight

Gentle whispers
like watercolor hues
of pale blue,
pink and peach

laughter paints
glittering colors
fuchsia, yellow,
or lavender hues

anger sprays,
deep red
magenta
and black

my rainbow
in tones
of hope
prismatic white

Child of the 70's

She grew up
without bicycle helmets,
car seats,
or bottled water.

When sticks and stones
could break your bones
but words
could not hurt –
but they did.

Words pricked her soul
like a tattoo needle
four eyes,
snob,
weirdo.

Words did hurt
but she never
raised a fist,
or her voice,
or a gun.

She tried to be invisible
but her body betrayed her
big boobs,
round hips,
cellulite.

Her body fodder,
for boys – and girls
speculation,
commentary,
envy.

Tending the Fire

just a spark
and fuel
and air
then flame

consumes, warms
comforts and rages
wildfire destruction
or welcoming hearth

glowing coals neglected
become ash—but
nurtured, fed, fanned
blaze to life

radiant cinders'
pulsing heat
reignite
offerings of tinder

torrid embers
banked
reawaken
with gentle breath

Seeing Red

Not the red
of anger and rage,
ink on a balance sheet,
or stop lights

but the deep crimson
of roses given to sweethearts,
velvet ribbons,
and Valentine cards

the warm red
of sun-ripened tomatoes
or weathered bricks

the sparkling scarlet
of radiant rubies,
well-aged merlot
and strawberry-stained lips

Oz

Landing in Oz
minus the technicolor
yearning to be Dorothy
and wear the magic shoes

Instead, I played the tin man
until my heart broke

pulling levers
behind the curtain
pretending to be
Great and Powerful

I never left Kansas

The Hammer

A woman
damaged by life
her heart beaten and battered
by men – and circumstance
like a bone-bruise
deeply injured
slow to heal

she took a hammer
to every new car
denting the glossy paint
marring the pristine surface
so, she was responsible
for the imperfection

she had only herself to blame

Broken Windshield Heart

how many hearts are broken
like a windshield
struck by a single stone
creeping cracks
slowly growing
from previous impact
eventually obscuring
the sight
of what lies ahead

Two Types of Pain

One pain
a dull ache
of a decaying tooth
building to
a knife edged crescendo
of agony
ebbing to nothingness
of a dead nerve
in an empty shell

the Other
the pain
of a shattered limb
amputated
leaving phantom nerves
aching and itching
at the memory
of what once
was there

All Injuries are Permanent

she was lucky, they said
the injury wasn't permanent
it was a lie

no visible scar
nothing to mar the skin
aesthetically intact

underneath fear lives
coiled and hissing
warning of danger passed

flashback memory
strikes in the dark –
all injuries are permanent

No Time to be a Victim

prying eyes and invading hands
unwanted advances, harsh words
insults, anger, and shame
all part of a past
things that cannot be erased

the pain lingers
in the back of the mind
demanding you be sad
to dwell – to grieve
to remain wounded, endlessly lamenting wrongs

tainted joy – toxic to the system
misery is a hungry beast
requiring nourishment
of heartache refreshed
to insure equilibrium and satiation

days, weeks, years of wallowing
epochs lost from bliss
surrendered power
to bullies
and daily tyrants

no more!
not another moment lost
to everyday despots, tormentors, or childhood abusers
take back life – and peace
with no time to be a victim

The Call

The call
expected
still shocks
two words

she's gone

grief and relief
the placeholder
where my sister
used to be

is gone

she left
bit by bit
hit by hit
lead away

by the high

no rock-bottom
just freefall
spinning
spiraling

away

The Shape of Grief

An amorphous blob
undefined, nebulous
enveloping you
in a straight-jacket
or a cocoon

A Fate Worse than Death

Death is a release
A divine nothingness
a warm and welcoming void

to those who live without hope
without joy,
without purpose or meaning

it is selfish grief
that mourns the liberated
and laments absence

for Death is a release
A divine nothingness,
a warm and welcoming void

Boxes of Anger

Where do you put the anger
when there is nobody to yell at
can you rage into a box
and bury it with the urn

who do you ask the questions
raised by an unfinished life
fury provides fire and warmth
in the desolation of loss

fire that tears could quench
but they refuse to fall

Winter Feelings

When you died, it was winter
for me it is winter still
glowing golden sun
wraps its rays around the verdant earth
like a mother embraces her child
nurturing it with her sultry embrace

sweat beads on my skin
as nature's hot breath bathes me
while frost clouds my sight,
and winter feelings congeal
only tears will thaw
the iceberg in my chest

Unforgotten
~for Vickie

It's like they have forgotten her already.
but they couldn't
how could anyone forget that laugh—
the one that burst like cannon fire
loud, exuberant, unrestrained
proclaiming "nothin' but love"

the joy that masked a well of hurt
the bravado that hid shame
the heart too open—too trusting
too willing to see the good in everyone—
even when it did not exist

maybe they remember too much

Dry Heat

the dry heat
of unshed tears
warms my morning coffee

staring out the window
seeing nothing
attention focused within

visiting them –
the ones that left
and the places gilded by memory

Timeline

For six weeks I was numb
I went to work, I shoveled snow
the next two months I was mad
I cleaned the house, I did laundry
for two more I was madder still
I weeded the garden, I washed the car
now, I cry.

The Weight of a Box

Four ounces of cardboard
and a plastic bag
hold twelve pounds of ash
from one hundred fifty pounds
of human remains
twelve pounds

What's Left Behind

I remember the museum exhibit "The Lives They Left Behind," featuring the suitcases discovered in the attic when they shut down Willard State Hospital, a mental institution. Everyday items hidden in the suitcases told the story of the patients who had lived, and died, within its walls. Photographs, books, and personal treasures—all clues to who they had been before they were crazy, before they died. Things carried from the world they knew. Things that were important to them. Things that they couldn't leave behind.

I remembered the exhibit as I sifted through your room and waded through the filth, clothes, and detritus that you lived in. Evidence of your own illness—drugs. I emptied drawers and found pills, straws, pipes—all things that you kept hidden, laying on photos of our grandparents. Photos that you clung to, but never cared for. Water-stained, sun-bleached, torn, but never discarded. Clothes that belonged to our mother, clothes you could never fit into, lay stained and trampled.

Then I looked at her. Your child, the one you could not let go, the one you pulled into your world of addiction, pain, and drama. The one with the mind of a child living in the body of a woman—a foot in both worlds, fitting in neither; she, like the clothes and photos, torn and trampled. I closed the door, left the things—and took her.

Laura Williams French is a poet, author, graphic designer and publisher. Laura received both her B.A. in cultural studies and her M.A. in English Literature from the State University of New York Empire State College. Laura lives in Upstate New York with her husband, daughter, niece, and three cats. Her book of humorous essays, *Wigs, Cars, and Sectional Sofas: Surviving Childhood in the 70's,* will be released in 2019.